Juel Andersen's

TOFU FANTASIES

A Cookbook of
Incomparable Desserts

A CREATIVE ARTS COMMUNICATIONS BOOK
Creative Arts Book Company

No part of this book may be used or reproduced in any manner
whatsoever without written permission from the publisher except in
the case of brief quotations embodied in articles or reviews.
ISBN 0-916870-44-8
Library of Congress Catalog Card No.: 81-71726

Creative Arts Books are published by Donald S. Ellis
For information contact
Creative Arts Book Company
833 Bancroft Way, Berkeley, CA 94710.

CONTENTS

APPLES WITH PRALINES

AND THE WORD: TOFU

The word TOFU is not in the dictionary. The closest my Webster's gets is "soybean" which is described as a ". . . legume, native to China and Japan but widely grown for its seeds, which contain much protein and oil, . . "

But tofu is not a "soybean," not at all. It is, as you know, the product of soybeans. It is made by milking those tiny beans with tiny fingers and making that milk into a sort of cheese that has become well known by now by its Japanese name: TOFU.

Tofu can be used as an ingredient in all sorts of good foods. It can be used in every meal of the day and in almost every kind of preparation. One of the most exciting ways to use tofu is as an ingredient in great desserts.

Some of the recipes in this collection may be familiar to you. You will notice, however, that such ingredients as cream cheese, butter, eggs, and sugar are used in reduced quantities or missing altogether. That's because you can make very risque confections with less of these things when you use tofu. You won't sacrifice either texture or taste, and you will feel very virtuous while you make a pig of yourself.

These desserts are not low calorie, just *lower* calorie. If you can *reduce* the calories in a recipe by substituting 1 pound of tofu (384 calories) for 1 pound of cream cheese (3,392 calories) that will be about 3000 calories for the entire recipe or about 300 calories a serving. Isn't that an impressive saving?

A discussion of the relative merits of sugar vs.

honey vs. other types of sweeteners does not enter my thoughts just now. Desserts are sweet, God bless 'em, and I love 'em. I am satisfied to cut down on the sweetener, not to replace it.

I hope you will have as much fun cooking these desserts as I did working out the recipes. And if the cooking is an adventure, wait until you taste them.

Why not begin with this one; it is "fantastisk godt" as we Danes say, and starts with "A" as for Apple.

APPLES WITH PRALINES

Pralines

1 cup walnut or pecan pieces
2/3 cup brown sugar
3 tablespoons water

Combine the brown sugar and water in a sauce pan and melt together, stirring for about 3 minutes after boiling begins. Grease a cake pan. Stir the nuts into the boiling sugar and pour the mixture into the greased pan. Allow to cool and harden. Break into chunks and chop with a knife into dime-sized chunks.

Apple Cream

8 large apples, or enough
  to make 6 cups of
  diced apple
Juice of one lemon
2 tablespoons butter
1/4 cup honey
1 teaspoon chopped or
  grated lemon peel
1 teaspoon vanilla
1/4 cup rum

1/3 cup water
1 tablespoon unflavored
  gelatin
1 cup soft tofu
1/2 cup unflavored
  yogurt
1/8 cup sugar
1/4 teaspon salt
1/8 teaspoon cinnamon
1 teaspoon vanilla

Peel, core, and dice the apples. Sprinkle with the lemon juice as you work to keep them from getting brown. Melt the butter in a heavy bottom saucepan and add the honey, apples and lemon peel. Cook these together, stirring frequently, until all moisture is gone and the apples are soft. Transfer to a mixing bowl and add the vanilla, rum, and 1/2 cup of the chopped praline mix.

Mix the gelatin with the water in a small pan. Stir over low heat until gelatin is melted. Stir this into the apple mixture.

Combine the tofu, yogurt, sugar, vanilla, salt, and cinnamon in a blender jar and beat until very smooth. Fold this into the cooled apple mixture. Spoon into individual glass serving dishes or into a beautiful glass bowl. Chill for at least 4 hours. Just before serving sprinkle the top with some of the praline mix, as much as you like.

8 servings

BABA AU RHUM
AND THE X-RATED COOKBOOK

We all hear the outcry against processed food. Not the kind that is whipped up in the home kitchen "food processor," but the kind that is presented to us, attractively packaged and seductively advertised by the giant corporations and their interlocking directorates.

For example, how many of you know that the Nestle Corporation includes the following products:

Taster's Choice
Libby, McNeill & Libby
Stouffer's
Decaf
Cross & Blackwell
Maggi
Swiss Knight Cheese
Deer Park Spring Water
Nestle's Crunch, Chocolate Chips, Quik, Nestea, Nescafe

There is also a fad for cooking and gratifying the palate. It must not be gratified greasily, nor gourmandily, but gourmetily and healthily.

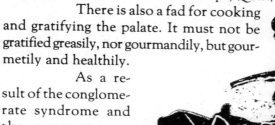

As a result of the conglomerate syndrome and the gourmet syndrome there are cookbooks of every persuasion and ethnic causality. These run from A for Algerian, through N for Natural, P for Pasta, right on to V for all sorts of Vegetarian. There is not, however, thus far, at this point in time, nor in this hemisphere, an X-rated cookbook of serious intent. I offer my little 2nd Reader of TOFU to fill the void.

To work up to the X-ratability I propose to start with a recipe for BABA AU RHUM. This fits in nicely as a transition to more intense culinary activities. This is because it is French in origin and uses a common potable, available in one of the highest alcohol titers known to man, 151 proof. If that isn't an adequate introduction to sin, nothing is!

BABA AU RHUM

1/2 cup dried currants
1/3 cup rum
1 tablespoon dry yeast
  (1 package)
1/4 cup warm water

1 teaspoon sugar
2 cups flour
1/2 cup butter or
  margarine
1/2 cup soft tofu

Wash the currants and set them to soak in the rum. Combine the yeast with the warm water and sugar. Set aside for about 5 minutes, until it foams. If it does *not* foam, the yeast is dead and you can stop right here, unless you have some good live yeast.

Cut the butter into the flour until it is the consistency of cornmeal. This can be done in a food processor or by hand with two knives or a pastry blender.

Combine the tofu and the yeast mixture. Beat this into the flour/shortening mix and beat and beat and beat, until the dough is verr-r-r-y elastic.

Place in a bowl, cover and let rise until doubled in bulk, about an hour.

Strain the currants, reserving the liquid for the sauce. Place the dough on a floured board and knead in the currants. Shape into a loaf and place in a 9" buttered bowl or deep pan. You may also form into small balls and bake in greased dariole molds or cupcake tins. Fill them to about half their volume. Cover the pan or molds and allow to rise again until doubled in bulk, about 45 minutes.

Bake at 400° for from 25 to 45 minutes, depending on size, until golden brown. Turn out immediately and cool on a rack.

Rum Sauce

1 1/2 cups water
1/2 cup sugar
Spices to taste:
  cinnamon stick,

nutmeg, anise, allspice.
1/2 cup 151 proof rum
  or other rum

Combine the water, sugar, and spices and boil until sugar is

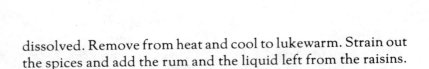

dissolved. Remove from heat and cool to lukewarm. Strain out the spices and add the rum and the liquid left from the raisins. Pour this syrup over warm or room-temperature babas, allowing them to soak up as much as they can.

Remove the babas with a slotted spoon and transfer to serving dishes or a platter. Reserve any left over syrup.

Serving

Serve the babas cold or at room temperature. Spoon a little of the syrup over them and top with whipped cream. If you have made just one large loaf, place it on a lovely plate, spoon syrup over it and top with whipped cream. Slice it at the table.

6-8 servings

CHOCOLATE CONCUPISCIENCE

AND ANOTHER WORD: SEXY

"You've got to make tofu sexy."

This is my husband calling long distance. "If you want to write a best seller cookbook its got to be sexy. I don't care what you say, just get tofu and sex together so I can quit working. Three tofu cookbooks already and where are we? Broke! Get busy. Find an angle. Make it SEXY! Okay? See ya Wednesday."

I think he must have been reading the book review section of the Sunday paper about how Shere Hite is making it big again with the latest news on sexuality.

"Okay, okay, I'll think of something!" He had already hung up.

So I've been doing a lot of thinking and trying to figure out a way to make my latest dessert concoction sexy. I thought of adding a special ingredient and the only one I could think of that has anything to do with sex was saltpeter. But I think that works some other way.

Then I looked for a little book I bought some time ago called "The Love Foods" which says under *soybeans* that "Orientals eat large quantities of soybeans and consider them a vital source of sexual virility." It did not say anything about tofu, but at least I had a lead now. But I still couldn't find the direction to go.

I called John back and said: "I'm not as good looking as Shere Hite and she's a lot younger." Who's she?" He sounded irritated. "What difference does it make how old you

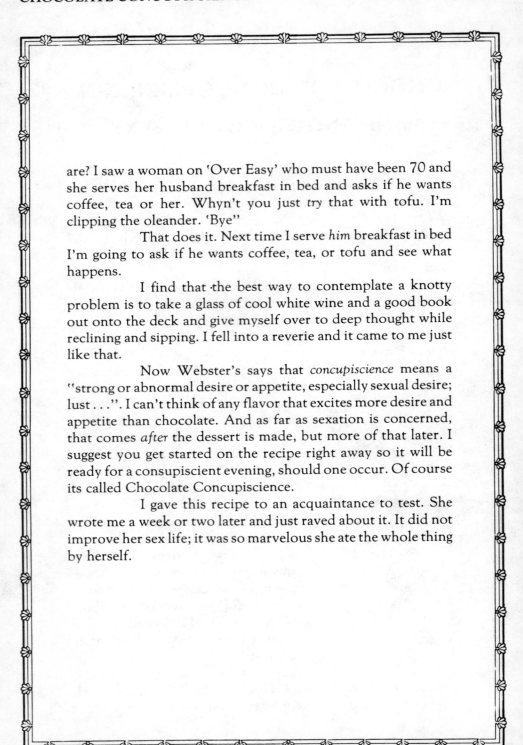

are? I saw a woman on 'Over Easy' who must have been 70 and she serves her husband breakfast in bed and asks if he wants coffee, tea or her. Whyn't you just *try* that with tofu. I'm clipping the oleander. 'Bye"

That does it. Next time I serve *him* breakfast in bed I'm going to ask if he wants coffee, tea, or tofu and see what happens.

I find that the best way to contemplate a knotty problem is to take a glass of cool white wine and a good book out onto the deck and give myself over to deep thought while reclining and sipping. I fell into a reverie and it came to me just like that.

Now Webster's says that *concupiscience* means a "strong or abnormal desire or appetite, especially sexual desire; lust...". I can't think of any flavor that excites more desire and appetite than chocolate. And as far as sexation is concerned, that comes *after* the dessert is made, but more of that later. I suggest you get started on the recipe right away so it will be ready for a consupiscient evening, should one occur. Of course its called Chocolate Concupiscience.

I gave this recipe to an acquaintance to test. She wrote me a week or two later and just raved about it. It did not improve her sex life; it was so marvelous she ate the whole thing by herself.

CHOCOLATE CONCUPISCIENCE

Crust

Preheat oven to 350°
1 cup crushed chocolate
  cookies

3 tablespoons oil or
  melted butter
1/2 cup chopped
  blanched almonds

Mix the cookie crumbs and the oil or butter together, blending well. Pat into a shallow mold with a capacity of 1 1/2 quarts. Bake at 350° for 10 minutes. While still hot, sprinkle the chopped nuts evenly over the baked crumbs. Cool on a rack.

Mousse Filling

1/2 pound bittersweet
  chocolate, grated
or 1 1/2 cups semi-
  sweet chocolate chips
1/4 cup water
2 tablespoons butter or
  oil
1 teaspoon instant coffee

1/2 cup cold water
1 tablespoon unflavored
  gelatin
1/4 cup Tia Maria, or
  Kahlua
1 cup soft tofu
1 teaspoon vanilla extract
Pinch of salt

Combine the chocolate, water, butter, and instant coffee in a heavy bottom pan and melt together over medium heat, stirring constantly until it is smooth and blended.

Moisten the gelatin with the cold water and add to the hot chocolate mixture, stirring until the gelatin melts completely. Remove from heat.

Combine the tofu, liqueur, vanilla, and salt in a blender or a food processor and start the machine. Add the chocolate mixture through the feed tube or the blender lid, stopping once or twice to scrape the sides of the container. Process until very smooth.

Pour this into the cooled crust. Refrigerate for several hours until set.

Chocolate Glaze

1/4 pound bittersweet chocolate
or 1/2 cup semi-sweet chocolate bits
2 tablespoons water

Combine the chocolate and water in a heavy bottom pan and stir over medium heat until melted and blended. If it is too thick to pour, add more water.

   Turn the chilled mold out onto a serving plate. This can be done by warming the mold slightly in warm water and running a flexible spatula around the edge of the crust. Pour the chocolate glaze over the inverted mold, allowing it to run over the top and down the sides of the dessert. Decorate with whole blanched almonds. Refrigerate until served.

   This delectable dessert can be frozen and served as a frozen confection. It can also be thawed and then served. It is perfect any way it is served and will satisfy the most intemperate chocolate lover.

P.S. My neighbor, Caroline has also tried this recipe. She is a chocolate freak, but does not discuss her sex life. She looks the same, but her husband is getting thinner. I don't think I need to say more about Chocolate Concupiscence.

WILD RIVER WHISKEY CAKE

AND CHOCOLATE SIN

Chocolate has been getting a lot of bad press lately. That probably accounts for the upsurge in its popularity. There is nothing like the association of a tad of sin to elevate even Ex-lax to soul food.

In 1896 there were a lot of people with some very elevated opinions of chocolate. They may have been misguided, but my friends Sylvia and George are not.

Sylvia has become an ardent tofu maker, even though she and George live about 7 miles from the nearest power pole and have a milk cow. I dedicated the following recipe to them and sent it along for testing. It calls for whipping cream and they have a lot of that too.

Sylvia and George live near a wild river in Northern California. They are not your usual dropouts, as they have neither long hair nor do they play the guitar. Sylvia used to be a dental assistant and George was a truck driver. They moved to the country to try out living like people did in the old days. Since there is no electricity, that immediately cuts out television, hi-fi, and a host of electronic amusements that most of us cannot live without. When I asked Sylvia what they do in the long evenings, she said they are becoming "very learned" because they read alot.

Since Sylvia learned to make tofu, she and George have lost about 16 pounds apiece. I won't hint that it had anything to do with tofu or the recipe for Wild River Whiskey Cake, but George, says they still find time to read.

WILD RIVER WHISKEY CAKE

1 package Stella D'Oro Anginetti or Lady Fingers
1/2 pound butter
1 cup semi-sweet chocolate bits
2 tablespoons cocoa
2 teaspoons instant coffee
2 teaspoons unflavored gelatin
1/3 cup boiling water
1/2 cup whiskey
1 cup (8 ounces) almond paste
2 cups soft tofu
1/2 cup sugar
2 teaspoons vanilla extract
2 teaspoons almond extract
1/2 cup coarsely chopped almonds
1 pint whipping cream (optional)

Melt the butter and chocolate together and add the cocoa and coffee powder. Melt the gelatin in the boiling water, cool slightly. Add 1/4 cup of the whiskey to the gelatin and set aside. Break the almond paste into bite sized chunks and place in a bowl. Pour the rest of the whiskey over them and stir gently. Set aside.

In a food processor or blender combine the tofu, sugar, vanilla, almond extract, and gelatin mixture. Blend until very smooth and then add the chocolate/butter mixture. Blend smooth again pour the mixture into a bowl. Add the almond paste by the spoonful, keeping it in lumps, stirring to distribute them evenly throughout the mixture. Stir in the chopped almonds.

Preparing the Mold

Lightly oil an 8″ or 9″ spring form. Split the Anginetti or lady fingers in two, crosswise, and line the bottom and sides of the pan. Don't worry about spaces between them, they will fill in with the whiskey mixture. Sprinkle them with Amaretto or Whiskey, very sparingly.

Pour the whiskey mixture into the mold. Refriger-

ate for several hours or overnight. Frost with whipped cream before serving.

The cake freezes well and can be served frozen or thawed. It is a most elegant dessert; a small slice is quite enough, if you can stop at that.

12 servings.

DUTCH TOFU DEVILS

AND COUPLES

Another interesting word to consider is "couple." The dictionary says it means to link two things, like railroad cars, pipe organ keys, lines of poetry, and people. Animals, too, can come in pairs, though they might not necessarily be referred to as a couple unless they are married.

One of the strangest couples I have seen lately is my little Schnauzer, Tofu, and his new playmate, an *enormous* St. Bernard named Dutch. Dutch's owner tells me that he is ordinarily indifferent to other dogs, but Tofu and Dutch struck up an instant and intense friendship and disappeared together for over three hours.

Tofu weighs just 18 pounds, which is slightly less than one of Dutch's legs. Dutch weighs 230 lbs. In spite of this great difference, they got along very well. When they finally returned from their hunting trip, Tofu was exhausted but raring to go on with the sport. I had to confine him and he cried pitifully for his monstrous friend, who circled the house for a full quarter hour until I drove him away. I haven't seen Dutch since.

My mind roves on to other couples among my own species no less startling. I ponder the basketball center type, 6'8" and all bone with his frau of 5'2" and wonder who he talks to in bed. Or I think on the man with the enormous beer belly against the wife with the enormous chest and imagine how they nest so neatly with complementary curves.

But far and above these amusing images stands that of my little Tofu and his giant new friend, Dutch, and to them I dedicate the next recipe: Dutch Tofu Devils.

DUTCH TOFU DEVILS

Preheat oven to 425°

Chocolate Squares

4 squares bitter chocolate
1/2 cup oil or butter
2/3 cup soft tofu
1 tablespoon instant
  coffee
2 teaspoons vanilla
  extract

1/2 teaspoon almond
  extract
1/4 teaspoon salt
1 1/2 cups sugar
1 cup all purpose flour
1 cup walnuts in large
  pieces

Melt the chocolate and oil (or butter) together over low heat or in the top of a double boiler.

Combine the tofu, coffee, vanilla, almond extract, salt, and sugar in a food processor or mixer bowl and mix very well. Add the flour and blend until just moistened. Add the slightly cooled chocolate mixture and mix well. Stir in the nuts.

Grease an 8″ square pan and dust with flour. Spread the chocolate mixture evenly in the pan. Lower the oven heat to 375° and bake the cake for 25 minutes, no more, no less. Remove to a rack and allow to stand for about 10 minutes. Loosen the cake with a spatula and turn out on a plate or another rack. Reverse immediately and allow to cool for several hours or overnight before cutting into squares.

makes 16 — 2″ x 2″ squares

Topping

for 8 servings

1 cup bittersweet chocolate bits
1/8 cup water
1 or 2 tablespoons rum, brandy or liqueur of
  choice (or more water)

Melt the chocolate in the water over a low flame. It should pour easily. Add liquor to thin.

To Serve

Chocolate squares (above)
Raspberry or other berry sherbert
Chocolate topping

Place a chocolate square in the center of a pretty plate. Place a nicely rounded scoop of sherbert on it. Spoon the topping over the sherbert and allow it to run down over the sides. It will harden almost immediately. Top with a single chocolate chip and serve.

VIKING CHOCOLATE CAKE

AND PERPETUAL YOUTH

Musing through the comic section of the Sunday paper I happened across Prince Valiant on my way to Doonesbury. My eye was caught by the words "Aleta is again with child . . . ."

Now, if memory serves, which it does with increasing indolence, Aleta is Mrs. Val and has been in a state of rampant fecundity for at least forty years. My servant, memory, catapulted me to childhood visits to Grandma who took the Chicago newspaper featuring Prince Valiant. The Prince was young then, even as I, and these visits to Grandma were prompted more by the chance to see the latest strip than by any love for my Old Granny and my maiden aunt, with whom she lived. They were always lying down, my Grandma on a bed and Aunt Rose on a studio couch which was covered with an Oriental rug. For all I knew, they had gone through life in that position.

My Aunt was the only woman I have ever known who could knit lying down. Grandma sighed a great deal, groaning "Gott im Himmel" to punctuate her suffering. My father was supposed to slip them a few dollars on the way out.

But back to Val and Aleta. Along with my adolescence they went through theirs. They married and, logically, ceased to age. I was not so fortunate and while I hardly remember my years of fecundity, I see Val and Aleta, while having weathered the storm of growing up, refuse to grow old.

Those treasured states: nubility, fecundity. Ah, the nostalgia it evokes. But what have these words to do with life and love and sex? Does Val still need his everlasting page-boy hair-do? Does Aleta need always to be flat all over? No siree, they don't. If both were really hip, Aleta would have formed a liason with a lately shipwrecked young bard from an out-king-dom. His name would be Valdor and he would strum a five string harp and relate tales of long ago, as much as 30 years ago, long before his birth. She would listen and smile and pretend that he was not 10 years younger than her son, and what difference would it make since she would still be handsome, still be blonde and still be, again, with child.

Val would be a hefty graybeard with a page-boy, and he would spend much of his time in the scullery with the chef, a young man of impeccable bearing. His name would be Lothar and he would cook such delicacies as this cake to please his master.

VIKING CHOCOLATE CAKE

Preheat oven to 350°
Oil two — 8″ layer cake pans

Cake

1/2 cup soft tofu
6 tablespoons cocoa
1/2 cup vegetable oil or
    melted butter
3/4 cup corn syrup
2 teaspoons instant
    coffee (optional)
1 cup buttermilk

2 teaspoons vanilla
    extract
1/4 salt
1/2 teaspoon baking
    soda
1 teaspoon baking
    powder
2 cups all purpose flour

Combine the tofu, cocoa, oil, syrup, coffee, buttermilk, vanilla, salt, soda, and baking powder in a mixing bowl or food processor. Mix until very smooth. Add flour and blend only until the flour is well mixed. Do not overbeat. Spread in the prepared pans and bake at 350° for about 30 minutes or until a toothpick comes out clean when inserted in the center of the cake. Cool on racks.

Coconut/Walnut Filling

1/2 cup soft tofu
1/3 cup melted butter
    or margarine (oil will
    not do)
3/4 cup confectioner's
    sugar
1 teaspoon vanilla
    extract

1/8 teaspoon salt
1/2 cup grated, flaked,
    or shredded *unsweetened* coconut
1/2 cup chopped
    walnuts

Combine the tofu and butter in a blender or food processor and blend very smooth. Remove to a bowl and stir in the sugar, vanilla, and salt, mixing well. Stir in the coconut and nuts. Refrigerate until spreading consistency, for 15 minutes or more. Spread between layers of the cake, or both between and

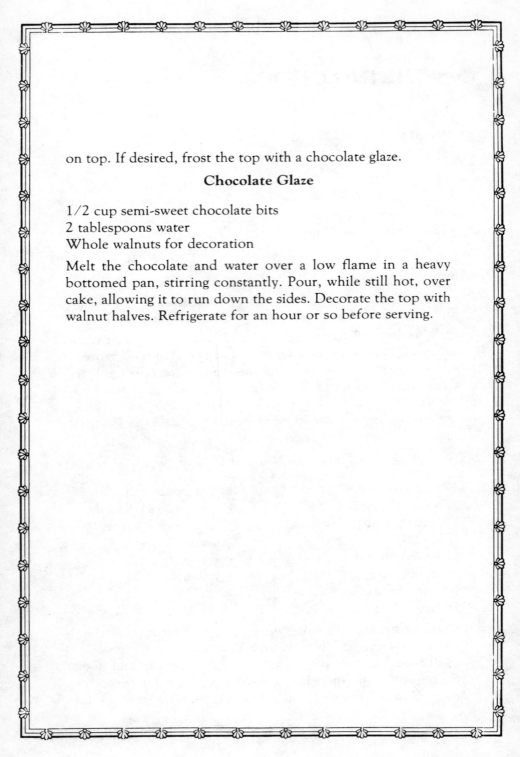

on top. If desired, frost the top with a chocolate glaze.

Chocolate Glaze

1/2 cup semi-sweet chocolate bits
2 tablespoons water
Whole walnuts for decoration

Melt the chocolate and water over a low flame in a heavy bottomed pan, stirring constantly. Pour, while still hot, over cake, allowing it to run down the sides. Decorate the top with walnut halves. Refrigerate for an hour or so before serving.

RASPBERRY FROMAGE

AND THE THERAPEUTIC FAST

I am sitting at my typewriter munching on Sunshine Biscuits tastiest snack cracker, Cheez-its. I have just finished another of those noble experiments in diet called the "therapeutic fast." It lasted 46 hours, 11 minutes and 22 seconds. It was broken with a large bowl of cottage cheese with yogurt, accompanied by a copious munch on the above named crackers. This will be followed by a quick trip to the nearest ice-cream purveyor for their jumbo single scoop of Mocha-Walnut-Fudge in a crunchy sugar cone. Then on to a cup of steamy coffee.

I know I am supposed to feel ashamed that I had not the fortitude and strength to see this thing through to the 48 hours I had set as my goal, but I just refuse. I don't feel ashamed, I feel downright silly to have begun fasting in the first place since I KNOW I'm going to fill all those empty spaces with the same kind of junk I had been eating for a long time before I ever heard of fasting.

I don't know why I permitted myself to be seduced by these latter day ascetics who indulge in stoicism and flailings with verbal scourges. Maybe I subscribe to too many kookie journals.

The therapeutic fast is supposed to cleanse your system, clear your eyes, and clean up your colon — once you get past the first few days. These are the difficult ones, the books say. But with steely determination and high minded thoughts it can be done. After those few days, it is all euphoria and enlightenment until you crash.

My problem is that I like to eat. I love to eat. I am addicted to food. It fulfills lots of needs. And I am not conditioned to self denial. I spent every waking moment of my mini-fast thinking of food and planning menus. I even fashioned a couple of new desserts. I dreamed of food at night, too, even some kinds I hate.

My love affair with tofu has nothing to do with self-denial. I am trying on every page of this book to make that clear. I just love to eat but I love eating desserts the most. Having found that tofu does double duty in making fantastic desserts and doing something good for myself, what more could I ask?

Now if you have found yourself in this predicament I have a suggestion. Once you have come down from your fast with plenty of Cheez-its and ice cream, try this recipe for something really lyrical, light, and sweet.

RASPBERRY FROMAGE

1 package frozen or 1
  pint fresh raspberries
2 tablespoons cold water
3 tablespoons lemon
  juice
1 1/2 tablespoons
  unflavored gelatin
1/2 cup boiling water
1/4 cup sugar, or to taste
1 cup soft tofu

1/2 cup buttermilk or
  unflavored yogurt
1 tablespoon Grand
  Marnier or other
  orange liqueur
1 teaspoon grated
  orange rind
3 egg whites
1/8 cup sugar
Pinch of salt
1/2 pint whipping cream
1 package Lady Fingers

Puree the raspberries in a blender and strain into a bowl. Set aside. Mix the cold water, lemon juice and gelatin together. Pour the boiling water over the dissolved gelatin mix and stir until the gelatin is melted. This can be heated gently if the gelatin does not melt completely.

Combine the sugar, tofu, buttermilk, liqueur, and orange rind in the blender and blend very smooth. Add the gelatin and pureed raspberries and mix again. Pour into a mixing bowl and refrigerate until set.

Prepare a mold for the mousse, either an 8″ or 9″ spring form or a bowl. If you use a bowl, oil it so the mold will release easily for serving. Line the mold with Lady Fingers.

When the mixture is set, begin by beating the egg whites until firm. Add the salt and 1/8 cup sugar gradually to make a fairly stiff meringue. Then beat 2/3 cup of whipping cream until stiff. Then beat the raspberry mixture until it is foamy and light. Fold in the whipped cream, then the meringue. Pour the mixture into the mold. Refrigerate several hours or overnight, until set.

To serve, remove the collar from the spring form or invert the mold on to a plate. You may serve with whipped cream or just as it is. In either case it is divine.

COCONUT TRIFLE

AND CUTTING UP IN ENGLAND AND WALES

My friend Kelly is like a new land to explore. She has so many facets and and so much life in her. She is cute and round and jolly and always smiles wryly at life and its comedy. She loves people and people love her.

Kelly's greatest love is traveling. She spent most of the last two years in and about the British Isles and did a great deal of cutting up.

For instance, she met two elderly spinster ladies, retired school teachers both, who had never done any spinning but were designated as such anyway. These ladies invited her to their retirement village — not Rossland or Larkmoor, but a real village on a real off-island. Kelly had a great time with these two, who were a cross between Margaret Rutherford and the Prince of Wales. One of their real problems was getting their hair cut. Kelly obliged with a neat trim for each.

"I've cut hair throughout Britain and Ireland, too, "says Kelly. "People are so grateful. Its such a little thing to do but its very personal."

Many of the stories she heard while the scissors snipped can't be shared, but a recipe can. This one is for a very fancy English Trifle. The Trifle is England's great contribution to the dessert art. It is a wonderful way to be frugal, using up all those old cookies and cakes that clutter up the pantry.

COCONUT TRIFLE

1 1/2 cups grated,
    unsweetened coconut
1/2 to 1 cup sweet
    sherry or sweet
    vermouth
1 cup milk
1/2 cup soft tofu
2 tablespoons lemon
    juice
1/2 teaspoon salt
1/4 cup sugar (plus
2 tablespoons for
    meringue)
1 teaspoon vanilla
1/4 teaspoon almond
    extract

2 tablespoons cornstarch
1 egg, separated
    (optional)
Slices of old yellow or
    white cake, or fresh
    cake, or cookies, or
    sponge cake or lady
    fingers or what have
    you.
1 — one pound can of
    fruit, well drained, or
    1 cup preserves or jam,
    any flavor you like, or
    fresh fruit or berries
1/2 pint whipping cream
1/2 cup chopped nuts

Spread the coconut on a baking sheet and toast in a 300° oven until lightly browned. Allow to cool.

Combine the milk, tofu, lemon juice, salt, sugar, vanilla, almond extract, and cornstarch in a blender and beat very smooth. Pour into a heavy bottomed saucepan and heat until it thickens. Beat in the egg yolk and remove from heat to cool.

Beat the egg white until stiff. Add 2 tablespoons of sugar to make a light meringue. Then fold into the cold custard. Refrigerate until you are ready to assemble the dish.

Assembling the Trifle

Line a deep glass dish or a spring form with the cake or cookies. Wet them with the sherry or vermouth, using only as much as you like or need. Spread a fairly thick layer of toasted coconut over the cake.

Pour some of the custard mixture over the coconut. Spoon in some fruit or preserves. Add another layer of cake or cookies. Sprinkle on more liquor. Spoon in more custard and more fruit very carefully. Add another layer of cake or cookies; then the rest of the custard and more fruit. Top with another layer of cake and sprinkle on the rest of the coconut. Add more liquor. Refrigerate for several hours, or overnight. To serve, turn out the mold or remove the rim from the spring form. Cut in wedges and top with whipped cream and a sprinkle of chopped nuts.

INCREDIBLE CAKE

AND OTHER CAPERS

There are some who would say that sex has no place in a recipe book, but I take issue with that notion. After all, sex is the counterpoint to daily life and nowhere in that round is sex more evident than in the kitchen.

Picture this. The door opens and Dick enters the kitchen. He is home from work; he is carrying a bouquet of roses and a box of chocolates. He sneaks up behind his wife, who has not heard him because the water is running.

He throws his arms around her in a loving embrace and whispers "Happy Anniversary, my darling!" "What did you say dear, you know I can't hear you with the water running," she yells, turning in his embrace. She begins to sneeze as they sink to the floor, he grappling with her panty hose. "You know I'm allergic to roses," she whines huskily. "Never mind, my love. Why are you wearing these things?" "They were on sale at the Safeway," she gasps.

"What's for dinner?" he asks, trying to be casual as his voice ascends an octave. "What's the goddamned combination to these pants?" "Hash," she answers, voice now husky. "Just pull down on the elastic. I know you hate hash, but I was so busy shopping for our anniversary."

There is then a piercing scream: "Lemme go,

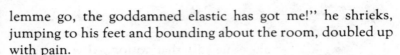

lemme go, the goddamned elastic has got me!'' he shrieks, jumping to his feet and bounding about the room, doubled up with pain.

So you see, sex does happen in kitchens.

However, had the scene been set properly, Jane would have been in the kitchen, yes, for young married women spend most of their time either cleaning in the kitchen or cleaning in the bathroom, or, occasionally, cleaning in the laundry room.

She would have been expecting Dick and would have been wearing the handsome negligee he had brought home the night before.

Jane hears the garage door open and rushes from the kitchen to the living room. There she quickly presses the switch to start the hi-fi, which softly begins to play ''their song.'' She sets a match to the kindling under the carefully set logs and quickly sinks to the white bear skin rug in front of the hearth. She only has time to arrange the black satin negligee to fall open exposing her naked thighs and naked everything else.

A single candle in a polished silver candlestick casts a flickering light on a spectacularly simple chocolate cake, low and glistening, decorated with one perfect pecan.

''Happy Anniversary, my darling,'' says Jane as Dick, in the process of throwing off his clothes, stumbles across the room.

''I would have brought roses, but I know you're allergic to them,'' he whispers, as he lowers himself beside her on the gleaming fur. ''What's for dinner?'' ''Nothing but me and this incredible Chocolate Cake,'' she murmurs huskily, indicating the cake with a limp wrist.

''That cake is incredible,'' says Dick, stroking her thighs. ''Just incredible! Did you buy it?'' He kisses her and sighs gently. ''No,'' she pants, ''I found the recipe in this little Tofu

Dessert Book. It's made with tofu. Isn't that incredible?"

"Yes, incredible!" exclaims Dick, breathing rapidly by now. He smooths her hair back from her damp brow and kisses her, dancing his tongue into her mouth, "What's the recipe?"

INCREDIBLE CHOCOLATE CAKE

Preheat oven to 350°
Prepare 3 8" layer cake pans with rounds of wax paper that are greased and dusted with flour.

Cake and Filling

6 squares unsweetened chocolate (6 oz.)
1/2 cup soft butter or margarine
2 1/2 cups confectioner's sugar
1 1/2 cups soft tofu
1 teaspoon instant coffee powder or crystals

2 tablespoons all purpose flour
1/2 teaspoon baking powder
1 teaspoon vanilla extract
8 egg whites or equivalent*
1/2 teaspoon salt
1/4 teaspoon cream of tartar

Melt the chocolate in the top of a double boiler. Combine the butter and confectioner's sugar in a food processor or mixing bowl and cream together until fluffy. Add the melted chocolate, tofu, coffee powder, flour, baking powder, and vanilla and beat until very smooth.

Beat the egg whites, salt, and cream of tartar until stiff. Fold into the chocolate mixture. Pour 1/4 of the batter into another bowl and refrigerate.

Divide the rest of the batter among the three prepared cake pans and bake at 350° for 15 minutes. Place on racks and cool completely.

Turn out the first layer on a cake plate. Remove wax paper. Frost with one-half of the reserved batter. Place the second layer on top. Be very careful as this cake is very delicate and breaks easily. Frost this with the other half of the reserved batter. Place the third layer on top. Refrigerate for several hours before finishing.

You can make a collar of wax paper to place around the layers to help it retain its shape. You can also use an 8" spring form to assemble the cake or just use the rim of the spring form.

Glaze

1/2 cup semi-sweet
  chocolate bits
2 tablespoons water or
  more

Walnut or pecan halves
or whole blanched
almonds

Combine the chocolate bits with the water in a heavy bottom pan and melt over slow heat, stirring to remove lumps and prevent sticking or burning. It should run freely when melted, if not add a bit more water, or a liqueur if you prefer. If it is too watery, cook longer to evaporate liquid. Pour this over the cold cake so that it runs down the sides. Decorate the top with nuts, as many as you like. Refrigerate for several hours or overnight before serving. If the plate is messy with chocolate, cut around the bottom edge of the cake with a sharp knife and place on another plate before serving.

       This cake freezes well. If frozen it should be served while still frozen or at refrigerator temperature. In any event, serve very cold.

*I often use dry egg white which can be rehydrated and beaten to a froth just as the fresh. 2 teaspoons + 2 tablespoons warm water = 1 egg white.

REED COLLEGE PEAR PIE

AND OTHER CEPHALIZATION OF THE STOMACH

Evolutionarily speaking, there is a tendency among animals for the nervous system to become concentrated in the head. A similar process might account for the gourmet complex that is so prevalent. It may be that the stomach, too, is also migrating upward and beginning to interfere with thought processes.

From former reading in psychology I remember a person named Penfield discovering during brain surgery, that electrical stimulation of certain areas caused patients to have visual hallucinations in vivid color. This was done 30 or 40 years ago.

It is my thesis that were those experiments conducted today the visual images would, without question, be of

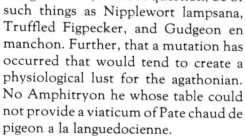

such things as Nipplewort lampsana, Truffled Figpecker, and Gudgeon en manchon. Further, that a mutation has occurred that would tend to create a physiological lust for the agathonian. No Amphitryon he whose table could not provide a viaticum of Pate chaud de pigeon a la languedocienne.

Admittedly, these are images that could not possibly occur to your "meat and potatoes" person. It is probably a development only possible in your high order intellectually oriented food connoisseur. But nonetheless valid.

To carry my thesis further, beyond Careme and Escoffier, the preparations named above would of necessity pale before those including TOFU in their list of ingredients. This is explained simply in terms of excessively rapid cephalization consequent upon the incorporation of this unequaled food into the gourmet repertoire.

As an example of this development I offer the following recipe which has its origins in one of the citadels of intellect on our West Coast. Strangely, there appears an anomalous ingredient, canned pears, but in view of the lofty intentions of the progenitors of the recipe, I offer it as related to me by Dr. J.E. Orr, with poetic alterations.

REED COLLEGE PEAR PIE

Crust

2 cups flour
1/2 teaspoon baking
  powder
1/2 teaspoon salt

1/3 cup oil
1/2 cup (1 cube) butter
1/3 cup ice water
  (or more)

Combine flour, baking powder and salt, mixing well. Blend in the oil. Cut in the cold butter, leaving pea sized lumps in the blend. Stir in the ice water until a ball is formed that leaves the sides of the bowl. Divide in two and roll the bottom crust on a floured board. Line the bottom of a 9″ or 10″ pie pan, glass preferred.

Filling

3 lbs. canned pears
  (1 29 oz. and
  1 16 oz. can)
1/2 cup sugar
1 tablespoon cornstarch
1/2 cup soft tofu
1/3 cup milk or butter-
  milk (or water)

2 tablespoons lemon juice
2 tablespoons canned
  orange juice concentrate
Pinch of salt
Nutmeg
Cinnamon
Butter for dotting

Drain the pears well, set aside. Combine the sugar, cornstarch, tofu, milk, lemon juice, and orange concentrate in the blender jar and blend very smooth.

Arrange pear halves in the bottom of pie crust. Pour cream mixture over the halves. Slice the rest of the pears and arrange the slices over the custard. Dot with butter and sprinkle with nutmeg and cinnamon to taste.

Roll out other half of crust and cover the pie. Crimp the edges and sprinkle crust with sugar.

Bake in a preheated 375° oven for about 25 minutes or until crust is nicely browned. Cool to room temperature before serving.

AMARETTO CREAM TORTE

AND THE ORGY

If you want instant orgy these days just say "Amaretto, m'love, on the rocks." This is a password to hot tubs, naked lunches, varieties of titilation, and intellectual smut of all kinds.

I was initiated to this world inadvertently. I was sipping grape soda at a Sierra Club forced march rest stop.

Someone had noted my grimace and asked what I would prefer to drink. I said, "Amaretto, m'love, on the rocks."

His eyebrows raised and lowered several times and he leered like a superannuated satyr. "I can help you to that very thing, m'dear, I'm having a small gathering at my place next Saturday. Do come."

The invitation was charming. "Wear anything at all," he called and he progressed up the trail, shoulders buoyant under his pack and mine.

I appeared at his pad the following Saturday. Little did I realize that my costume was just right for the proceedings. It is always difficult to decide what to wear in the San Francisco area. Temperatures vary from early ice age to tertian Sahara within a mile or two or a minute and a half. I have this wondeful dress, which can go from one to the other climate and back again by adding or subtracting undergarments.

It was a scorching June day, unusual in Marin, and I arrived sans all but this dress — long, loose, and flowing. Before I could greet my host, I was catapulted out of the dress and into a hot tub with a glass of Amaretto over ice in one hand, wet hair in the other, and an assortment of fingers, toes, and tongues in every available orifice. I hardly had time to set down the impressive dessert I had brought.

"Have you read the latest Hite Report?" I asked when my mouth was suddenly disengaged. "Bug off," someone said. "Yeah, stuff her," said someone else.

I was free again and shouted. "Watch out for my left breast, I just had a biopsy." "Talk, talk, talk," mumbled someone else, "all these new ones do is talk."

I brought an Amaretto Cream Torte," I managed to gasp. "Where is it?" was the chant, in unison, and everyone jumped out of the tub. Here is the recipe:

AMARETTO CREAM TORTE

Amaretto Cream

2 tablespoons plain
  gelatin (2 packages)
1 cup cold water
1/2 cup butter
(1/4 pound) or 1/2 cup
  bland oil
3/4 cup sugar
1/4 teaspoon salt
1 tablespoon vanilla
  extract
1/2 tsp. almond
  extract

1/2 cup milk
2 cups very fresh,
  soft tofu
1/4 cup Amaretto
  Liqueur
1/2 pint heavy cream
  (optional)
1/2 cup blanched
  almonds
1 package frozen rasp-
  berries or other berries

Dissolve the gelatin in the water. Combine the gelatin mixture, butter, sugar, and salt in a saucepan and cook over low heat, stirring constantly, until melted together.

Combine the vanilla, almond extract, milk, tofu, and Amaretto in a blender jar or food processor bowl and mix until very smooth. Add the gelatin mixture, while blending. Pour into a glass or stainless steel bowl and refrigerate until set.

Preparing the Mold

1 package Lady Fingers
An 8″ or 9″ spring form

Oil the spring form with a light coating. Line the sides and bottom with lady finger halves.

If you are using the heavy cream, whip it until it is fairly stiff. Whip the set gelatin mixture at high speed until it is frothy and light. Fold in the whipped cream.

Pour this into the prepared spring form and refrigerate for several hours or overnight.

Serving

The torte is served with toasted almonds and a spoonful of berry puree. Chop the almonds until the pieces are the size of corn kernels. (Do not use a blender or food processor for this. You will end up with almond meal.) Brown these in the oven at 350° checking and stirring them often so they will not burn.

Put the berries through a food mill or coarse strainer to remove the seeds. Bring to a simmer over medium heat and cook until the volume is reduced by half. This makes a puree of intense flavor; very little need be used.

Before serving, remove the wall of the spring form and place the mold on a serving dish. Sprinkle the toasted almonds over the top. Serve the berry puree in a small pitcher with a tiny ladle, so that you can serve your guests or they can help themselves.

10 to 12 servings

AMERICAN LEMON CHEESE CAKE
AND THE MORAL MAJORITY

Sex is not for everyone and that's a fact. Sometimes it can be an embarrassment, and this is especially so with the young. If you ask most teenagers how they feel about the thought that their parents actually "did it" they are likely to get very red and say, "Yeah, —once."

If you ask middled aged persons the same question they will be distinctly uncomfortable with the thought that their aged parents did it once and may still do it.

If you protest that *you* certainly do not feel that way, never did, and what's more, can't even understand such an attitude, you are probably lying.

But considering middle America and the moral majority and such conservative thinkers, it might be well to pause here and insert a recipe that can't offend anyone. It is so American, so moral, so righteous, I could cry. But in spite of its monumental sobriety, it is very good tasting. Exceptionally good tasting. And quick and easy. And made with *cake mix.*

AMERICAN LEMON CHEESE CAKE

Preheat oven to 350°

Crust

1 package Pudding
  Cake Mix
1 egg yolk (save white for
  filling)

1 tablespoon lemon juice
1/2 teaspoon lemon peel
1/3 cup oil

Measure out 1 cup of cake mix and set aside. Measure the rest of
the mix (3 cups) into a mixing bowl. Mix the egg yolk, lemon
juice, lemon peel, and oil together and add to the cake mix,
blending with a fork or the fingers. Grease a 9″ x 13″ pan and
pat the mixture into the pan. Bake at 350° for 10 minutes.
Remove to a rack until filling is ready.

Filling

1 1/2 cups soft tofu
2 ounces sharp cheddar
  cheese
1/4 cup oil
2 tablespoons cornstarch
1/3 cup lemon juice

1/2 cup plain yogurt
1/3 cup sugar
1/2 teaspoon salt
  (optional)
Remainder of cake mix
2 eggs, separated

Combine the tofu, cheese, oil, cornstarch, lemon juice, yogurt,
sugar, salt, and egg yolk in a blender or food processor and
blend until very smooth.

Transfer to a mixing bowl, add the remaining cake
mix and beat for 2 full minutes. Beat the egg whites until stiff
and fold into the batter. Spread this over the partially cooled
crust and bake at 350° for 35 minutes. Cool before serving.

12 to 15 servings

GRASSHOPPER PIE
AND THE GOLD COUNTRY

One of the strange sights in California is the summer landscape of parched hills peopled only by live oak trees. Visitors from Mars and Indiana find this a most distressing scene, but distress visits the San Franciscan and other cosmopolites in other guises.

A drive through the fabled "gold country" on State Route 49 takes you through one little town after another, all of them displaying store signs in a kind of broken lettering style I call *Sour-Dough Gothic*.

The route is crammed with antique shops featuring refinished oak furniture imported from New England and Old England and other points East. The prices boggle the mind. There are also folksy little restaurants serving sandwiches and other things made with whole grains and sprouts and tofu and other foods our ancestors knew nothing about. The clothing shops feature authentic gold-panner overalls, bandanas, straw hats, and sunbonnets. The hardware emporiums sell gold panning kits with complete instructions.

In between towns, are the hills, and the pick-up trucks. The latter are driven at very slow speeds by cigarette-smoking natives wearing wide-brimmed straw hats of Western curl. You see this through the windows, from behind. There is also, generally, a female head in silhouette and images of several smaller heads hopping about in disarray. These apparently belong to immature members of the species.

Bellishing is the pastime of the business people in these many gold towns, upbellishing and downbellishing as well as em-. But behind the facade and the trading is the real California that can never be changed: the poetry of the yellow hills, the drama of the canyons, and the charm of the inexorable sunshine, matters of geography untainted by the hand of commerce.

In honor of that real California and my windshield I offer this recipe for Grasshopper Pie.

GRASSHOPPER PIE

Preheat oven to 350°

Crust

4 tablespoons butter, margarine or oil
1 1/4 cups chocolate crumbs from cookies or dry cake

Melt the butter and combine with the chocolate crumbs. Pat into a 9″ pie pan. Bake at 350° for 7 minutes. Cool on a rack while preparing the filling. Reduce oven temperature to 300°.

Filling

1 1/2 cups soft tofu
2 tablespoons lemon juice
2 tablespoons cornstarch
2/3 cup sugar
1/2 cup buttermilk or thin yogurt
1/4 cup vegetable oil

1/4 teaspoon salt
1 teaspoon vanilla
1/4 cup green Creme de Menthe (or white + 3 drops green food color)
2 teaspoons white Creme de Cacao

Combine all the filling ingredients in a blender jar or food processor and whip until very smooth. Pour into the chocolate crumb crust. Bake at 300° for about 30 minutes, until almost set. Test with a knife, which should come out not quite clean. Cool and then top with either Chocolate Tofu Creme or Chocolate Sour Cream as follows:

Chocolate Tofu Creme

1/4 cup butter or margarine
1/2 cup semi-sweet chocolate bits (4 oz.)
3/4 cup soft tofu

1 tablespoon sugar
1 tablespoon cocoa
2 teaspoons lemon juice
1 teaspoon vanilla
Pinch of salt

Melt the butter and chocolate together and cool slightly. Combine the tofu, sugar, cocoa, lemon juice, vanilla, and salt in a blender or food processor and blend very smooth. Add the chocolate and blend smooth again. Spread over the cooled grasshopper pie. Refrigerate until firm. *Do not bake.*

Chocolate Sour Cream

1/2 cup semi-sweet chocolate bits
2 tablespoons water
1/2 cup sour cream

Melt the chocolate bits with the water and cool. Mix with the sour cream and pour over the cooled grasshopper pie. Refrigerate until firm.

8 servings

CHOCOLATE INDIFFERENCE
AND KEEPING *AU COURANT*

It is possible to place the most delectable chocolate dessert in front of some people and find no more reaction than a Bassett hound to a martini. No one can look as profoundly bored as a Bassett hound, unless it is a person indifferent to chocolate.

According to an article I read not long ago, food has taken precedence over sex and politics as a "provocative conversational subject" in many "elevated social circles." Chocolate is high on the list of subjects, being the "trendiest of flavors." Though the authentic French spelling of the world is "chocolat," some of the most effete have dropped the "h" in order to be the most inner of the most elevated.

But I say, and I say it emphatically: *the most elevated conversations in any circle take place among persons who are indifferent to chocolate.* These are not chocolate haters, or chocolate dislikers. These are the ones who, when given the choice, take vanilla or strawberry ice cream instead of Chocolate Incandesence. They take lemon pudding before Cocolat Stridence. They will eat naked toffee rather than a Chocolat Impertinence.

There will be one or two of them at all social gatherings. They will find one another as soon as dessert is served.

"I'll take the strawberry tarte," one whispers de-

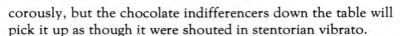

corously, but the chocolate indifferencers down the table will pick it up as though it were shouted in stentorian vibrato.

"I'll take the other one!" another shouts from down the board.

"And I too," chimes in a latecomer. "But they're all gone!!"

"Do not be alarmed," soothes the hostess. "We had anticipated this newest trend, it is called Chocolate Indifference and I have copies of the recipe for you to take home." And this is how the copy read:

CHOCOLATE INDIFFERENCE*

Preheat oven to 425°

Crust

1 1/4 cups all purpose
  flour
1/2 teaspoon baking
  powder
1/2 teaspoon salt
1 tablespoon sugar

1/4 cup oil
1/2 stick (1/4 cup)
  frozen butter
1/4 cup soft tofu
1 tablespoon milk

Combine the dry ingredients and mix well. Blend in the oil. Cut the butter in 1/4″ chunks and cut into the flour mixture. Blend in the tofu with a pastry fork, adding the milk by droplets, to form a very soft dough. Press into a 10″ or 11″ tart pan and prebake in a 425° oven for 10 minutes, or until it begins to brown. Remove to a rack to cool while you prepare the fillings. You can glaze the crust with warmed, very thick apricot jam before filling, if you wish. This will help to keep the crust crisp.

Reduce oven to 350°

Filling

The filling can be any fresh fruit or well drained canned fruit. Fresh peach slices, fresh apricot halves, fresh Italian plum halves, fresh sweet cherries, apple slices, or berries are all delicious. Spread them evenly over the prepared crust, in one layer. If the fruit is very tart, sprinkle the crust with one tablespoon of sugar before adding the fruit.

Custard

2/3 cup buttermilk
1/2 cup soft tofu
1/4 cup oil or softened
  butter

1/4 cup sugar
2 teaspoons cornstarch
2 tablespoons lemon
  juice

Combine in a blender jar and beat until very smooth. Add sugar to taste, if the fruit is very tart. Pour the mixture over the fruit in the prepared crust and bake at 350° for 20 minutes. If the fruit is not soft, bake for another ten minutes. Cool on a rack. Serve the tart at room temperature or slightly warm. If you like cinnamon, a fine dusting is appropriate. You may give up chocolate after you taste this tart.

* or Fruit Tart

MINCE PIE

AND THE SYLLOGISM

Aristotle is known as the father of the syllogism. This is a proposition that says, mathematically:

if $A = B$
and $C = A$
then $A = C$

The whole proposition hinges on that little word "if" because that is your basic assumption. Now, if:

Tofu is my dog
and   Some dogs are named Tofu
then   My dog is some dog

I think that follows quite well. Now if:

Tofu eats with Dutch
and   a St. Bernard eats with Tofu
then   Dutch is a St. Bernard
         or does Dutch eat tofu?
         or is Tofu a St. Bernard?

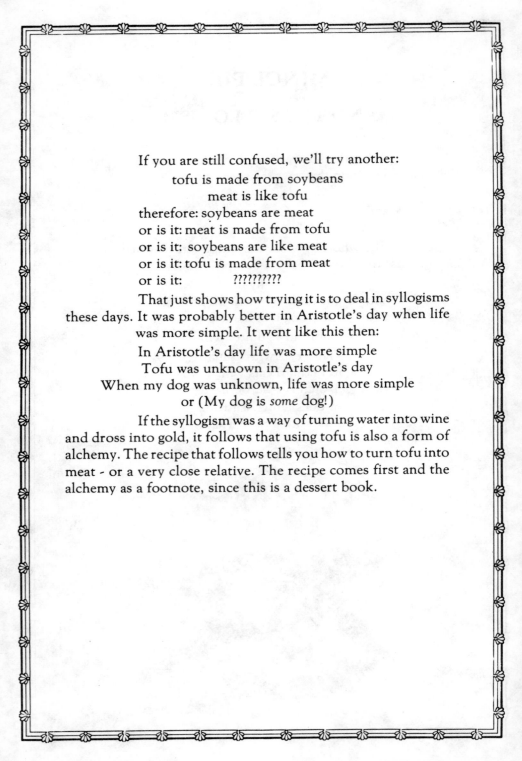

If you are still confused, we'll try another:

tofu is made from soybeans
meat is like tofu
therefore: soybeans are meat
or is it: meat is made from tofu
or is it: soybeans are like meat
or is it: tofu is made from meat
or is it: ??????????

That just shows how trying it is to deal in syllogisms these days. It was probably better in Aristotle's day when life was more simple. It went like this then:

In Aristotle's day life was more simple
Tofu was unknown in Aristotle's day
When my dog was unknown, life was more simple
or (My dog is *some* dog!)

If the syllogism was a way of turning water into wine and dross into gold, it follows that using tofu is also a form of alchemy. The recipe that follows tells you how to turn tofu into meat - or a very close relative. The recipe comes first and the alchemy as a footnote, since this is a dessert book.

MINCE PIE

Mincemeat

1 cup thawed, flaked tofu
   or 2/3 cup PSP (see
   Tofu Alchemy page
   00) rehydrated in 1
   cup boiling apple juice
   or cider
1/4 pound, or 1/2 cup
   butter, oil or
   margarine
1/2 cup dried currants
1 1/2 cups raisins
3 cups chopped apple
   (about 4 medium
   apples)

2 tablespoons chopped
   lemon rind
2 tablespoon chopped
   orange rind
3/4 cup brown sugar or
   honey
2 tablespoons molasses
1 1/2 cups apple juice
1/2 teaspoon each of
   cinnamon, mace,
   ground cloves
1/4 teaspoon each of
   nutmeg, ground all-
   spice, ground anise,
   salt
1/3 cup brandy or rum

Combine all the ingredients, except the brandy in a heavy bottomed saucepan and cook for an hour or more, until all liquid is evaporated and the apples are soft. Stir in the liquor and store in a sealed jar, in the refrigerator for a week or more before using.

makes 1 quart

Pie Crust

2 cups all purpose flour
1/2 teaspoon baking
   powder
1/2 teaspoon salt

3/4 to 1 cup shortening
1/3 to 1/2 cup ice water
   or very cold milk

Mix the flour, baking powder and salt. Cut in the shortening with a pastry fork or two knives, or use the food processor according to directions in its handbook. More shortening will make a crust with a softer crumb, so use the amount you like.

Stir in the ice water using a table knife blade, until the pastry leaves the sides of the bowl. Divide the dough into two parts, one larger than the other. Use the larger portion for the bottom crust. Roll out on a floured board or cloth or between two sheets of wax paper. Line an 8″ or 9″ or 10″ pie pan.

Mince Pie

You can use the mincemeat as it is, or if you prefer it to be milder add:

        1 to 2 cups fresh, chopped apple
        1 cup chopped walnuts or pecans

Fill the bottom crust just level with the rim. Top with a full crust or with lattice crust. Sprinkle with sugar. Bake in a preheated 425° oven for about 15 minutes, then reduce the heat to 325° and continue baking for about 30 minutes, until crust is golden brown and pie juices are thick.

Place on a rack. Serve warm or at room temperature with hard sauce or a scoop of ice cream.

TOFU ALCHEMY
(HOW TO TURN EXTRA TOFU, LEFT OVER TOFU, AND OLD TOFU INTO A WHOLE NEW FOOD)

Reviving Old Tofu

Cut into chunks, cover with water, boil for 10 to 20 minutes. Use as you would fresh tofu or freeze it. Boiling will change texture, making it tougher and chewier. It will no longer be suitable for desserts, excepting mince meat.

Saving Tofu

If you have tofu you will not be using, put it in the freezer in a plastic bag, either dry or with water. Save it until you need it.

Thawing Tofu

Thaw in the refrigerator overnight or at room temperature for several hours. You can also submerge it in tepid water and speed up the process. Press out water by squeezing in a towel or by wrapping it in paper towels and putting a weight on it.

Using Thawed Tofu

1. Cube and deep fry for croutons or use in dishes instead of meat.
2. Crumble and use instead of meat in dishes calling for ground meat. Especially MINCE MEAT.

Making PSP

PSP stand for Processed Soy Protein. It is very like the textured vegetable protein you can buy, but much better. Better because you make it yourself from thawed tofu. Press the water from thawed tofu; crumble it to pieces the size of rice kernels; mix it with a flavoring such as strong bouillon or tamari (1 tablespoon to 1 cup crumbled tofu); spread it on a cookie sheet and dry it in a 275° oven for about an hour. It can be dried in a food dehydrator, on a wood stove or radiator, or in the sun just as well. Store it in a closed container. It will keep for about a

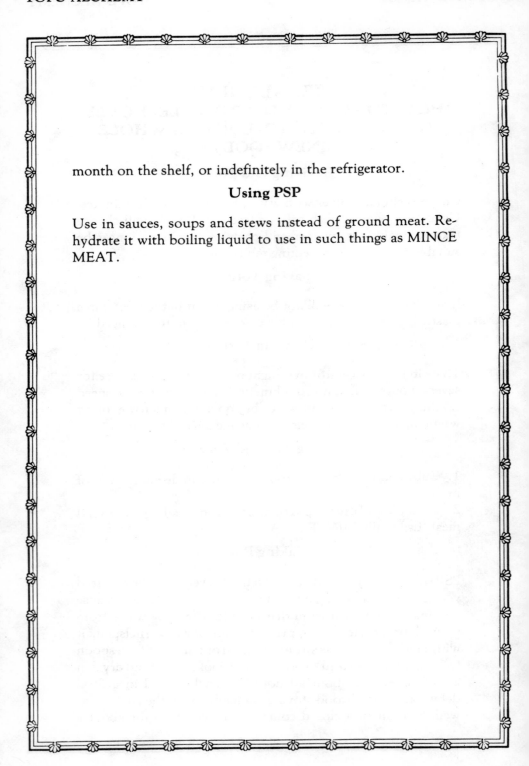

month on the shelf, or indefinitely in the refrigerator.

Using PSP

Use in sauces, soups and stews instead of ground meat. Re-hydrate it with boiling liquid to use in such things as MINCE MEAT.

CHOCOLATE AND VANILLA CHEESECAKE

AND OTHER CHEESECAKE

"Great, great, Othello! Yeah, right on. Okay. Okay. Lift your elbow and show the cufflike. Oh God, that's great! Look under the brows, look macho-like. Yeah. Okay. Beautiful, Othello. Lift the shoulder. Yeah. Beautiful. Okay, Othello, thats it! Thanks."

In its own context the above makes a kind of sense. It is the patter of a photographer cudgeling one of the beautiful people in New York to make with the elegant pose. Othello is the "professional" name of a model. He is among the dozens of models who appear seductively in full color photographs in the proliferating mail order catalogs that make daily transit from my Post Office box to the waste basket.

It seems that a whole generation of stylized poseurs have been produced by that notorious photograph of Truman Capote which appeared long ago on the jacket of his first best selling novel. He posed recumbent, propped on one elbow, pouting, and looking at the world from under his eyebrows. The "underbrow pout" has become ubiquitous. The heartbreak is that there are so many, many, beautiful underbrow pouters nowadays, and so few slick magazines. The models are stumbling over each other in heated competition for high status jobs.

My information came from an overlong documentary about New York models. One must wonder at the mentality that makes going through phoney antics in front of a lens the be-all and end-all to a good many young Americans. It also gives one pause to note the voracious appetite the model agencies have for babies; not the kind in diapers, but the emotional kind who could as well be playing jump-rope and jacks as sitting still for hours while skilled cosmeticians transform them into demimondaines. It is outrageous to rush children into precocious sexuality when the world is overpopulated as it is. But, I have forgotten that sex is now a recreative, not procreative, activity in the view of many young folk.

The part of the documentary that got to me showed one of these incredibly beautiful babies posing for head shots in a ruffled collar, two hours of paint, and an encouraging underbrow pout. She kept moving her head to the coos of the photographer, the click of the shutter and the winding of the film. As she smiled and raised and lowered her eyebrows, went from a pout to a mischievous leer, she was unmistakably mouthing the word "cheese."

Now the mouthing of the word "cheese" goes back a hundred years or more, to the very beginning of photography. It is astonishing and ludicrous to think that we have not advanced to mouthing "fromage" or "ost" or "cuesa" when in many other endeavors we have advanced the cause by giving the mundane a foreign name. For example, we now call meat loaf, "pate," and get wild response.

But, of course, the mouthing of the word: "cheese" goes beyond culinary purpose. It, indeed, is a very sexy ma-

neuver of the mouth. When said aloud it has other connota-
tions, not the least of which, when attached to another vocal,
evokes visions of delight. That vocal is "cake" or "pie." We all
know what photographic "cheesecake" is, and thus far, it has
been the subject of our discourse. But now I turn to a healthier
cheesecake, the kind that is consumed in a literal way. I offer
this recipe, not as a substitute for 13 year olds in lustful pose,
but as an anodyne for those who do not have one within reach.

CHOCOLATE AND VANILLA CHEESECAKE

Preheat oven to 350°

Crust

1 cup chocolate cookie crumbs
1 tablespoon honey
3 tablespoons melted butter or oil

Crush the cookies to make fine crumbs. Mix with the honey, allowing the honey to pour in a fine stream while mixing. Blend in the butter or oil with a fork. Spread the mixture in a 9″ or 10″ pie pan or spring form and bake at 350° for 10 minutes. Cool while preparing the filling.

Cheese Filling

3 eggs, separated
3 ounces Swiss or
  Cheddar Cheese
1/3 cup melted butter,
  margarine or oil
1/3 cup yogurt

1 cup soft tofu
1/2 cup sugar
2 teaspoons vanilla
1 tablespoon vinegar
1/2 teaspoon salt
3 tablespoons flour

Combine the eggs, cheese, butter and yogurt in a food processor or blender and beat until very smooth. Add the tofu, sugar, vanilla, vinegar, salt and flour and blend again, until very smooth. Remove 1/2 cup of the mixture to use with chocolate.

      Beat the egg whites until stiff and fold into the cheese mixture.

Chocolate Filling

1/2 cup semi-sweet chocolate bits
2 tablespoons butter
1/2 cup cheese mixture (from above recipe)

Melt the chocolate and butter together. Cool slightly and then beat in the reserved cheese mixture.

Pour the vanilla cheese mixture into the baked crumb crust and smooth it with a spatula. Drop large spoonfuls of the chocolate mixture into the vanilla mixture in about six places around the pie. *Do not stir the chocolate, unless you want a marbled effect.* There should be well defined areas of black and white.

Bake at 350° for about 20 minutes, until the sides puff. The center will be quite soft. Cool on a rack and then refrigerate for several hours before serving.

10 to 12 servings

INDEX

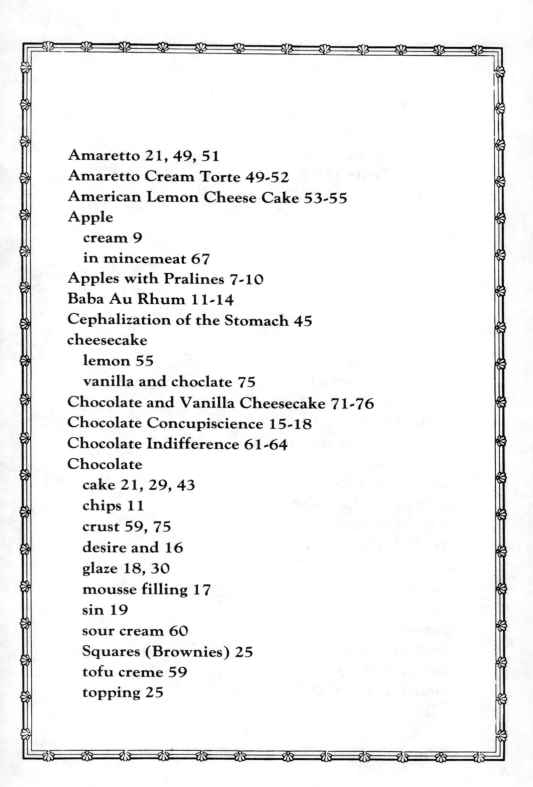

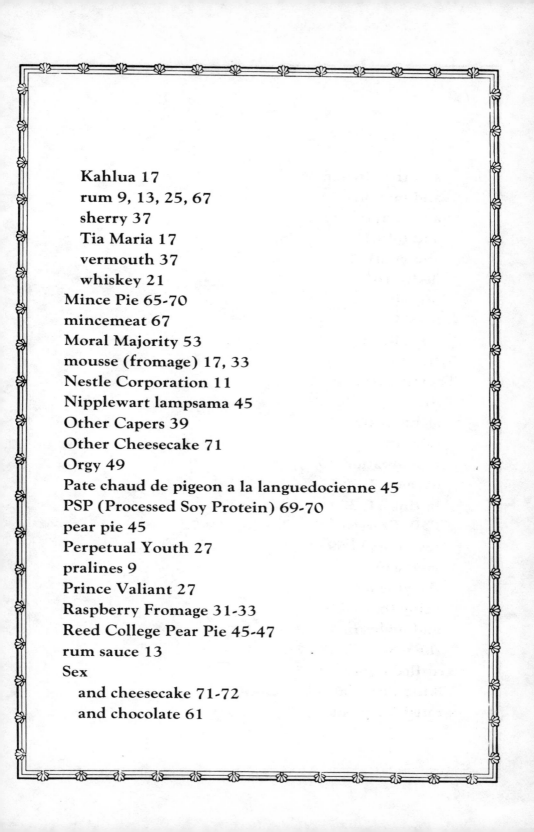

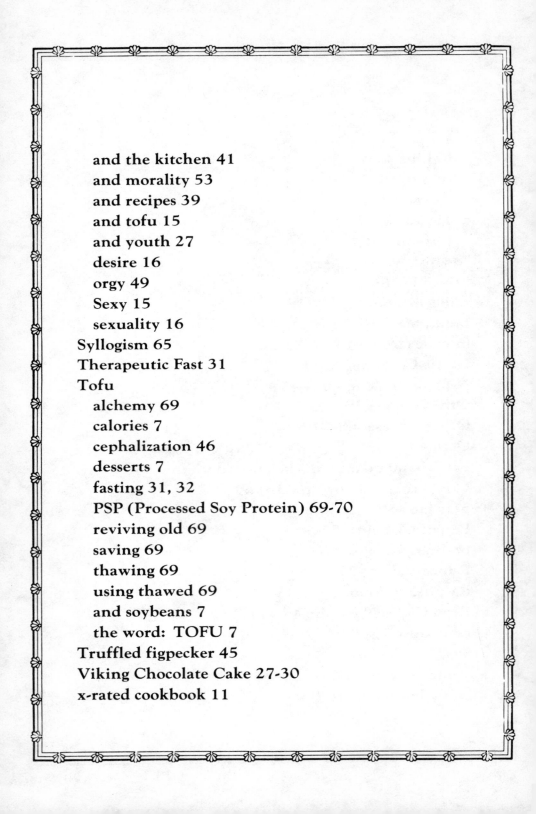

ABOUT THE AUTHOR

TOFU FANTASIES is Juel Andersen's fourth book of TOFU recipes, and it is the one she likes best. If you like to cook, if you like to read, and, especially, if you like to eat DESSERTS, you will like it too.

"Most people are wok-happy when it comes to cooking with tofu. When they hear that I write tofu cookbooks they always tell me about their latest stir-fry recipe. I tell them to hide their woks and get out their blenders and try something new!"

In this book you will find Juel's answer to Chocolate Decadence. It is called CHOCOLATE CONCUPISCIENCE. Also presented are INCREDIBLE CAKE, which is, enigmatically, both baked and unbaked; MINCE PIE, made with mince and without meat; CHOCOLATE INDIFFERENCE, a tart for those who do not swoon over chocolate; and a batch of other delights. Juel has prefaced the desserts with some spicy comments that may make this the first X-rated cookbook with *real* recipes.

A refugee from the Middle West, Juel Andersen has lived and worked in California for 25 years. She has been a psychologist, a teacher, a wife, a mother, a goldsmith, and a writer of cookbooks, in that order. She lives and works in a small town in the Sierra Nevada mountains.

Her books are *The Tofu Cookbook* (Rodale Press, 1979), *The Tofu Primer* (Creative Arts, 1980), *Juel Andersen's Tofu Kitchen* (Bantam Books, 1982) and this volume. "I'm a tofu-cooker or maybe a tofuer;" Juel says, "it's an adventure in cooking that anyone can have." She has also designed and is marketing *Juel Andersen's Tofu Kit* a complete guide for making tofu in your own kitchen.

"I never expected tofu to become another career, but one thing leads to another and I can't stop now. I think tofu is the food of the 80's and will find its place as a standard food item as did yogurt and sour cream. It is exceedingly deserving since it is more versatile, lower calorie, cholesterol-free and inexpensive."

THE TOFU PRIMER

A Beginner's Book of Bean Cake Cookery
Juel Andersen with Sigrid Andersen

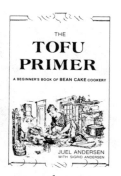

The first ABC of Tofu cooking, *The Tofu Primer*, charmingly illustrated with drawings from early 1900s children's books and an 1853 French cookbook, presents Tofu (soybean curd) in the most imaginative guises conceivable for use in every meal. High in protein, low in calories, containing no cholesterol, tofu's versatility as an ingredient is unparalleled, replacing, as it does: eggs, oil, mayonnaise, sour cream and milk products. Tofu has been a staple in the diet of the people of Japan since the 10th century, having been imported from China, where it is known as "the meat without bones."

This ancient protein food is taking its place in the American diet as well, not only for its food value but as something of an economic miracle. Widely available now in supermarkets and natural food stores, tofu can also be made at home, as illustrated in *The Tofu Primer*. An invaluable investment for everyone!

Copies of *The Tofu Primer* can be ordered by sending $3.00 + $1.00 postage and handling to:

CREATIVE ARTS BOOK CO.
833 Bancroft Way
Berkeley, California 94710